Life Grammar Through Pictures

Keep Your Students Talking

A Typical Day

Joyce A. Cook

Illustrations by: Lauren Segarra

A Typical Day

DEDICATION

Dedicated to all the many students from more than 60 different countries that I have had the pleasure of teaching for over 35 years and the many teachers that I have trained. I pray that many more teachers will be helped by using the Life Skill books to teach Internationals to conquer their fear of learning the English language.

ACKNOWLEDGMENTS

Thanks to God for giving me the passion and gift to teach English. Thanks to Lauren for doing the excellent illustrations for this book and to my encouragers: Dave, Dale, Leslie and Marie for giving me the confidence to write and publish these Life Skill and Grammar books. I pray that some of my teaching skills will live on through other teachers who possess that same passion to teach English to both Immigrants and Refugees coming into our great Country, the United States of America.

CONTENTS

"Life Skills and Grammar Through Pictures"
Keep Your Students Talking

How to use this book:
It's very important in an ESL class, that the student should do most of the talking, not the teacher. This book will help you do just that. In each Chapter there is a life skill taught and at the same time they are learning grammar skills by just looking at pictures and verbal repetition.

This "tool" is to be used along side other things, it is not supposed to be the only thing the students will use in the class. If your class is 2 hours, only use 1 hour in this book. The students love the repetition. They need to hear just 1 word about 50 times before it is written solidly in their brains. This book uses complete sentences not just words so repetition is very important. Below is a sample as to how to use repetition while learning different tenses of verbs, adding adverbs or adjectives to them, etc.

I believe you will find this book not only useful but a great learning tool for your students. It can be used one on one or in a classroom setting. I have used this concept for many years and have never had a student that did not enjoy learning English using this method. Each class is different and adjusting each lesson to meet your needs is very important.

Lesson Example: (This is only an example; feel free to adjust as needed for your students.)

Sequence 1:
- Teacher pronounces the sentence and the students repeat while only looking at the pictures. (3 times each.)
  Mother wakes up at 6:00.

- Teacher pronounces and students repeat 3 times each for #2.
  She turns off the alarm clock.

- Teacher returns to #1 and repeats it one time.
- Teacher then repeats #2 once again one time.
- Teacher than goes to #3 and say it 3 times with students repeating it after each time.

She gets out of bed.

- Teacher returns to #1 and repeats it one time.
- Teacher then repeats #2 once again one time.
- Teacher then repeats #3 once again one time.
- Teacher than goes to #4 and says it 3 times with students repeating it after each time.
  She puts on her robe.

- Continue doing this through the entire 8 pictures. Then have the students say it without your assistance unless needed. If there is more than one student, have the first student say #1, the second #2, etc… Repeat changing students each time until you are sure the students have a good grasp of the sentences.

- Once the students understand the sentences using "She" then change to using "I". By changing from "She" to "I", this will also change the verb tense. For example "Mother *wakes* up at 6 AM" to "I *wake* up at 6 AM." The teacher will say the new sentence first with the students repeating only once. Continue using the different tenses through all 8 pictures until each student understands and can repeat the new sentences using "I" with the proper tense of the verb.

- The third time going through the sentences/pictures, have the students add "every morning" to the end of each. Go through using "She" then "I" adding "every morning" at the end of each sentence. Repeat this until you feel the students are pronouncing it correctly.

- The fourth time going through the sentences/pictures, change the sentences to negative sentences following the same method as before. For example: "Mother **wakes** up at 6 AM" to "Mother **does not** *(or doesn't, good time to teach contractions)* **wake** up at 6 AM."

- The last time going through the sentences/pictures, have the students change each sentence from a statement to a question, for example: "Mother wakes up at 6 AM" to "Does mother wake up at 6 AM?"

I believe you will find this method works well and the students learn and are doing most of the talking. It takes about 1 hour to go through the above plan using all the pictures in one sequence if you have about 6 students and they are all about the same level. You may need to adjust how much you accomplish in one class setting.

Each unit can also be taught on two different days. Let them get the grasp of what each picture represents then move on to changing things. Again, you know your students, so move along at their pace. Do not move on until all the students have grasped each skill. If you need to stay on one sequence or only do half of one sequence for another class, that's ok. Giving the students the confidence to speak looking at only the picture is the main purpose of this book.

Chapter 1

Preparing Child
for School

SEQUENCE 1:

SEQUENCE 2:

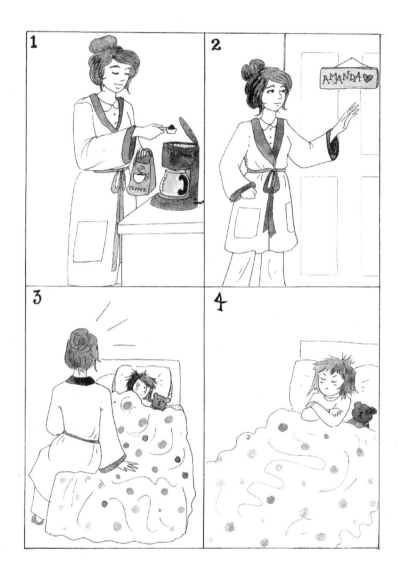

SEQUENCE 3:

SEQUENCE 4:

Chapter 1- Preparing Child for School

Sequence 1:
1. Mother wakes up at 6:00.
2. She turns off the alarm clock.
3. She gets out of bed.
4. She puts on her robe.
5. She goes to the bathroom.
6. She washes her face.
7. She brushes her hair.
8. She goes to the kitchen.

Sequence 2:
1. She makes coffee.
2. She goes to Amanda's bedroom.
3. She wakes up Amanda.
4. Amanda does not want to wake up.
5. Mother pulls back the covers.
6. Amanda gets out of bed.
7. Mother returns to the kitchen.
8. Amanda dresses for school.

Sequence 3:
1. Mother cooks breakfast.
2. She sets the table.
3. She pours the milk.
4. She calls Amanda to eat.
5. Amanda comes to the table.
6. Amanda eats her breakfast.
7. She thanks her mother.
8. She hugs her mother.

Sequence 4:
1. Amanda puts on her coat.
2. She gets her books.
3. She gets her lunch.
4. She walks to the bus stop.
5. Mother looks out the door.
6. Amanda talks to her friends.

7. The bus is at the bus stop.
8. Amanda waves good bye.

More Practice Work for Chapter one using the same pictures.

Sequence 1: *(Note, this can be repeated for all 4 sequences.)*
Change Mother to I.
1. Mother wakes up at 6:00.
   I wake up at 6:00.
2. She turns off the alarm clock.
   I turn off the alarm clock.
3. She gets out of bed.
   I get out of bed.
4. She puts on her robe.
   I put on my robe.
5. She goes to the bathroom.
   I go to the bathroom.
6. She washes her face.
   I wash my face.
7. She brushes her hair.
   I brush my hair.
8. She goes to the kitchen.
   I go to the kitchen.

Sequence 2: *(Note, this can be repeated for all 4 sequences.)*
End each sentence with *every morning.*
1. She makes coffee *every morning.*
2. She goes to Amanda's bedroom *every morning.*
3. She wakes up Amanda *every morning.*
4. Amanda does not want to wake up *every morning.*
5. Mother pulls back the covers *every morning.*
6. Amanda gets out of bed *every morning.*
7. Mother returns to the kitchen *every morning.*
8. Amanda dresses for school *every morning.*

Sequence 3: *(Note, this can be repeated for all 4 sequences.)*
Change each sentence to a negative sentence.

1. Mother cooks breakfast.
    Mother doesn't cook breakfast.
2. She sets the table.
    She doesn't set the table.
3. She pours the milk.
    She doesn't pour milk.
4. She calls Amanda to eat.
    She doesn't call Amanda to eat.
5. Amanda comes to the table.
    Amanda doesn't come to the table.
6. Amanda eats her breakfast.
    Amanda doesn't come to the table.
7. She thanks her mother.
    Amanda doesn't thank her mother.
8. She hugs her mother.
    She doesn't hug her mother.

Sequence 4: *(Note, this can be repeated for all 4 sequences.)*
Change each sentence with a question with *'you'*.

1. Amanda puts on her coat.
    Do you put on your coat?
2. She gets her books.
    Do you get your books?
3. She gets her lunch.
    Do you get your lunch?
4. She walks to the bus stop.
    Do you walk to the bus stop?
5. Mother looks out the door.
    Do you look out the door?
6. Amanda talks to her friends.
    Do you talk to your friends?
7. The bus is at the bus stop.
    Are you at the bus stop?
8. Amanda waves good bye.
    Do you wave good bye?

MORE CONVERSATION:

1. What time do you get up?
2. Do your children get up early?
3. Are they easy to get out of bed?
4. What do they eat for breakfast?
5. Do they ride a school bus?

Chapter 2

Typical School Day

SEQUENCE 1:

SEQUENCE 2:

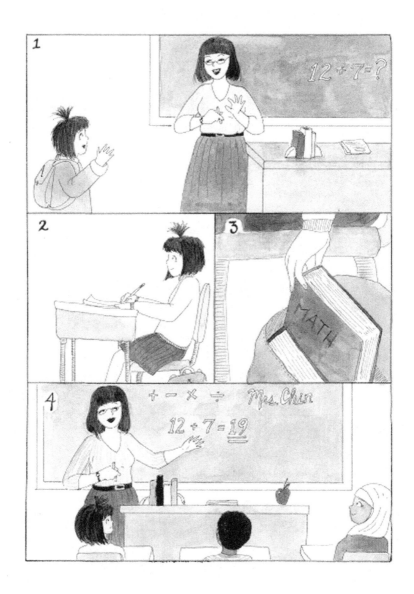

SEQUENCE 3:

SEQUENCE 4:

Chapter 2 – Typical School Day

Sequence 1:
1. Amanda gets on the bus.
2. She sits with her best friend, Stephanie.
3. She talks about school.
4. She gets off the bus.
5. She enters the school.
6. She opens her locker.
7. She finds her books.
8. She walks into the classroom.

Sequence 2:
1. She says good morning to her Teacher.
2. She sits at her desk.
3. She takes out her math book.
4. Mrs. Chin teaches them math.
5. Amanda finishes her math paper.
6. She gives the teacher her paper.
7. She reads while the other students finish.
8. Amanda has recess for thirty minutes.

Sequence 3:
1. Amanda likes recess.
2. She plays ball with her friend, Stephanie.
3. Tommy tries to take their ball.
4. He wants to play too.
5. They let Tommy play too.
6. Mrs. Chin rings the bell.
7. Our Recess is over.
8. They return to their classroom.

Sequence 4:
1. Amanda likes school.
2. Mrs. Chin is a good teacher.
3. English is her favorite subject.
4. It is time for their lunch.
5. The students line up.
6. They walk to the lunch room.
7. The lunch room smells good.

8. Amanda enjoys her lunch.

More Practice Work for Chapter two using the same pictures.

Sequence 1: (*Note, this can be repeated for all 4 sequences.*)
Change Amanda to I.
1. Amanda gets on the bus.
   I get on the bus.
2. She sits with her best friend, Stephanie.
   I sit with my best friend, Stephanie.
3. She talks about school.
   I talk about school.
4. She gets off the bus.
   I get off the bus.
5. She enters the school.
   I enter the school.
6. She opens her locker.
   I open my locker.
7. She finds her books.
   I find my books.
8. She walks into the classroom.
   I walk into the classroom.

Sequence 2: (*Note, this can be repeated for all 4 sequences.*)
End each sentence with "everyday." Then begin each sentence with "Everyday."
1. She says good morning to her Teacher, Mrs. Chin.
   She says good morning to her Teacher, Mrs. Chin everyday.
   Everyday, she says good morning to her Teacher, Mrs. Chin.
2. She sits at her desk.
   She sits at her desk everyday.
   Everyday, she sits at her desk.
3. She takes out her math book.
   She takes out her math book everyday.
   Everyday, she takes out her math book.
4. Mrs. Chin teaches them math.
   Mrs. Chin teaches them math everyday.
   Everyday, Mrs. Chin teaches them math.

1. Amanda finishes her math paper.
    Amanda finishes her math paper everyday.
    Everyday, Amanda finishes her math paper.
2. She gives the teacher her paper.
    She gives the teacher her paper everyday.
    Everyday, she gives the teacher her paper.
3. She reads while the other students finish.
    She reads while the other students finish everyday.
    Everyday, she reads while the other students finish.
4. Recess lasts thirty minutes.
    Recess lasts thirty minutes everyday.
    Everyday, recess lasts thirty minutes.

Sequence 3: (*Note, this can be repeated for all 4 sequences.*)
Change each sentence to a negative sentence. Then change each to a negative sentence using "I."
1. Amanda likes recess.
    Amanda doesn't like recess.
    I don't like recess.
2. She plays ball with her friend, Stephanie.
    She doesn't play ball with Stephanie.
    I don't play ball with Stephanie.
3. Tommy tries to take their ball.
    Tommy doesn't try to take their ball.
    I don't try to take their ball.
4. He wants to play too.
    He doesn't want to play.
    I don't want to play.
5. They let Tommy play too.
    They don't let Tommy play.
    I don't let Tommy play.
6. Mrs. Chin rings the bell.
    Mrs. Chin doesn't ring the bell.
    I don't ring the bell.
7. Our Recess is over.
    Recess is not over.
    My recess is not over.
8. They return to their classroom.
    They do not return to their classroom.
    I do not return to my classroom.

Sequence 4: (*Note, this can be repeated for all 4 sequences.*)
Change each sentence to a question. Then change each to a question using "I."

1. Amanda likes school.
    Does Amanda like school?
    Do I like school?
2. Mrs. Chin is a good teacher.
    Is Mrs. Chin a good teacher?
    Am I a good teacher?
3. English is her favorite subject.
    Is English your favorite subject?
    Is English my favorite subject?
4. It is time for their lunch.
    Is it time for lunch?
    Is it time for my lunch?
5. The students line up.
    Do the students line up?
    Do I line up?
6. They walk to the lunch room.
    Do they walk to the lunch room?
    Do I walk to the lunch room?
7. Their lunch room smells good.
    Does their lunch room smell good?
    Does my lunch room smell good?
8. Amanda enjoys her lunch.
    Does Amanda enjoy her lunch?
    Do I enjoy my lunch?

MORE CONVERSATION:

1. Do your children like riding the bus?
2. What is their favorite subject in school?
3. Do you know their friends at school?
4. Do they like their teachers?
5. Do they pack their lunch or eat school lunches?

Chapter 3

Typical Day for Mother

SEQUENCE 1:

SEQUENCE 2:

SEQUENCE 3:

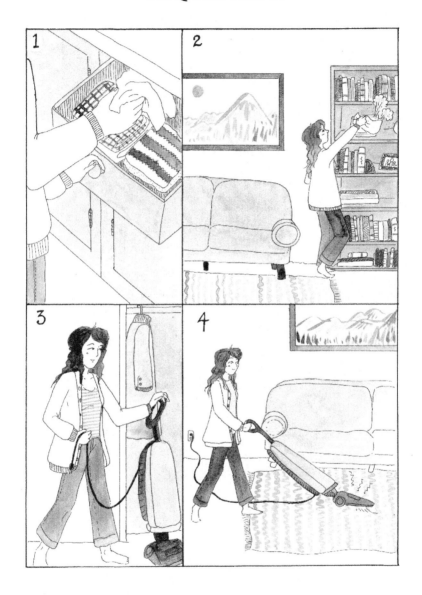

SEQUENCE 4:

Chapter 3 – Typical Day for Mother

Sequence 1:
1. Mother closes the front door.
2. She goes to the kitchen.
3. She washes the breakfast dishes.
4. She sweeps the kitchen floor.
5. She sits at the table.
6. She plans her day.
7. She plans dinner.
8. She writes a grocery list.

Sequence 2:
1. She goes to her bathroom.
2. She takes a shower.
3. She dries off with a towel.
4. She puts on her bathrobe.
5. She dries her hair.
6. She puts on her clothes.
7. She cleans the bathroom.
8. She goes downstairs.

Sequence 3:
1. She takes out her dust cloth.
2. She dusts the living room.
3. She takes out her vacuum cleaner.
4. She vacuums the living room.
5. She goes to the laundry room.
6. She puts clothes in the washer.
7. She puts clothes from the washer to the dryer.
8. She folds the dry clothes.

Sequence 4:
1. She fixes her lunch.
2. She eats her lunch.
3. She goes up stairs.
4. She makes the beds.
5. She goes to the kitchen.
6. She prepares dinner.

7. She puts the dinner in the oven.
8. The kitchen smells good.

More Practice Work for Chapter three using the same pictures.

Sequence 1: (*Note, this can be repeated for all 4 sequences.*)
Change Mother to I.

1. Mother closes the front door.
   I close the front door.
2. She goes to the kitchen.
   I go to the kitchen.
3. She washes the breakfast dishes.
   I wash the breakfast dishes.
4. She sweeps the kitchen floor.
   I sweep the kitchen floor.
5. She sits at the table.
   I sit at the table.
6. She plans her day.
   I plan my day.
7. She plans dinner.
   I plan dinner.
8. She writes a grocery list.
   I write a grocery list.

Sequence 2: (*Note, this can be repeated for all 4 sequences.*)
End each sentence with "everyday." Then begin each sentence with "Everyday."

1. She goes to her bathroom.
   She goes to her bathroom everyday.
   Everyday, she goes to her bathroom.
2. She takes a shower.
   She takes a shower everyday.
   Everyday, she takes a shower.
3. She dries off with a towel.
   She dries off with a towel everyday.
   Everyday, she dries off with a towel.

4. She puts on her bathrobe.
   She puts on her bathrobe everyday.
   Everyday, she puts on her bathrobe.
5. She dries her hair
   She dries her hair everyday.
   Everyday, she dries her hair.
6. She puts on her clothes.
   She puts on her clothes everyday.
   Everyday, she puts on her clothes.
7. She cleans the bathroom.
   She cleans the bathroom everyday.
   Everyday, she cleans the bathroom.
8. She goes downstairs.
   She goes downstairs everyday.
   Everyday, she goes downstairs.

Sequence 3: *(Note, this can be repeated for all 4 sequences.)*

Change each sentence to a negative sentence. Then change each to a negative sentence using "I."

1. She takes out her dust cloth.
   She doesn't take out her dust cloth.
   I don't take out my dust cloth.
2. She dusts the living room.
   She doesn't dust the living room.
   I don't dust the living room.
3. She takes out her vacuum cleaner.
   She doesn't take out her vacuum cleaner.
   I don't take out my vacuum cleaner.
4. She vacuums the living room..
   She doesn't vacuum the living room.
   I don't vacuum the living room.
5. She goes to the laundry room.
   She doesn't go to the laundry room.
   I don't go to the laundry room.
6. She puts clothes in the washer.
   She doesn't put the clothes in the washer.
   I don't put the clothes in the washer.
7. She puts clothes from the washer to the dryer.
   She doesn't put clothes from the washer to the dryer.
   I don't put the clothes from the washer to the dryer.

8. She folds the dry clothes.

> *She doesn't fold the clothes.*
> *I don't fold the clothes.*

Sequence 4: *(Note, this can be repeated for all 4 sequences.)*
Combine sentences to make compound sentences using "She" and "I" and a conjunction "and."

1. She fixes her lunch..
2. She eats her lunch.

> *She fixes her lunch and eats her lunch. (Replace "her lunch" with "it" the second time around. Explain using a pronoun first.)*
> *I fix my lunch and eat it.*

3. She goes upstairs.
4. She makes the beds.

> *She goes upstairs and makes the beds.*
> *I go upstairs and make the beds.*

5. She goes to the kitchen.
6. She prepares dinner.

> *She goes to the kitchen and prepares dinner.*
> *I go to the kitchen and prepare dinner.*

7. She puts the dinner in the oven.
8. The kitchen smells good.

> *She puts dinner in the oven and the kitchen smells good.*
> *I put dinner in the oven and the kitchen smells good.*

MORE CONVERSATION:

1. Is it quiet when your children leave for school?
2. What do you do when your children are at school?
4. What time do you fix dinner?
4. What day of the week do you wash laundry?
5. Do you typically stay home all day?

Chapter 4

After School and Bedtime Routine

SEQUENCE 1:

SEQUENCE 2:

SEQUENCE 3:

SEQUENCE 4:

Chapter 4- After School Routine

Sequence 1:
1. Amanda gets out of school.
2. She rides the bus home.
3. Mother meets her at the bus stop.
4. They go into the house.
5. Mother gives Amanda her snack.
6. Mother reminds Amanda to do her homework.
7. Amanda finishes her homework.
8. Amanda wants to play outside.

Sequence 2:
1. Amanda has to clean her room first.
2. She cleans her room.
3. She goes outside to ride her bike.
4. Her friend, Bobby, is riding his bike too.
5. They ride to the park.
6. They play at the park for 15 minutes.
7. They ride back to their house.
9. Mother says that it's almost time for dinner.

Sequence 3:
1. Amanda washes her hands for dinner.
2. Father comes home from work.
3. Amanda is so happy to see him.
4. They all go to the table.
5. Father blesses the food.
6. They all enjoy the meal.
7. Mother clears the table.
8. Amanda helps mother with the dishes.

Sequence 4:
1. The family watches TV.
2. Amanda takes her bath.
3. She puts on her pajamas.
4. She gets out her clothes for the next day.
5. She shows father her homework.
6. She prepares her back pack for school.

7. She kisses her mother and father goodnight.
8. She gets in bed.

More Practice Work for Chapter four using the same pictures.

Sequence 1: (*Note, this can be repeated for all 4 sequences.*)
Change Amanda to I, me, my, or we.
1. Amanda gets out of school.
   I get out of school.
2. She rides the bus home.
   I ride the bus home.
3. Mother meets her at the bus stop.
   Mother meets me at the bus stop.
4. They go into the house.
   We go into the house.
5. Mother gives Amanda her snack.
   Mother gives me my snack.
6. Mother reminds Amanda to do her homework.
   Mother reminds me to do my homework.
7. Amanda finishes her homework.
   I finish my homework.
8. Amanda wants to play outside.
   I want to play outside.

Sequence 2: (*Note, this can be repeated for all 4 sequences.*)
End each sentence with *every day*.
1. Amanda has to clean her room first *every day*.
2. She cleans her room *every day*.
3. She goes outside to ride her bike *every day*.
4. Her friend, Bobby, is riding his bike too *every day*.
5. They ride to the park *every day*.
6. They play at the park for 15 minutes *every day*.
7. They ride back to their house *every day*.
8. Mother says that it's almost time for dinner *every day*.

Sequence 3 *(Note, this can be repeated for all 4 sequences.)*
Change each sentence to a negative sentence.
1. Amanda washes her hands for dinner.
   Amanda doesn't wash her hands for dinner.
2. Father comes home from work.
   Father doesn't come home from work.
3. Amanda is so happy to see him.
   Amanda isn't so happy to see him.
4. They all go to the table.
   They all don't go to the table.
5. Father blesses the food.
   Father doesn't bless the food.
6. They all enjoy the meal.
   They all don't enjoy the meal.
7. Mother clears the table.
   Mother doesn't clear the table.
8. Amanda helps mother with the dishes.
   Amanda doesn't help mother with the dishes.

Sequence 4: *(Note, this can be repeated for all 4 sequences.)*
Change each sentence to a compound sentence using "and then."
1. The family watches TV.
2. Amanda takes her bath.
   The family watches TV and then takes her bath.
3. She puts on her pajamas.
4. She gets out her clothes for the next day
   She puts on her pajamas and then gets out her clothes for the next day.
5. She shows father her homework.
6. She prepares her back pack for school.
   She shows father her homework and then prepares her back pack for school.
7. She kisses her mother and father goodnight.
8. She gets in bed.
   She kisses her mother and father goodnight and then gets in bed.

MORE CONVERSATION:

1. Do your children ride a school bus?
2. What time do they get home?
3. Do they get snacks after school?
4. Do they have homework everyday?
5. What time do you eat dinner everyday?

Chapter 5

Typical Saturday
Routine

SEQUENCE 1:

SEQUENCE 2:

SEQUENCE 3:

SEQUENCE 4:

Chapter 5- Typical Saturday Routine

Sequence 1:
1. Amanda wakes up.
2. She jumps out of bed.
3. She goes to the bathroom.
4. She goes to the kitchen.
5. Father cooks breakfast.
6. Amanda hugs her Father.
7. She sits at the table.
8. She eats pancakes.

Sequence 2:
1. Amanda cleans the breakfast dishes.
2. Mother takes Amanda to the mall.
3. They shop for new shoes.
4. They have lunch in the food court,
5. They drive home.
6. Amanda shows Father her new shoes.
7. Father and Amanda go to the park.
8. They get their ball gloves.

Sequence 3:
1. Amanda plays on the swing.
2. Amanda and Father play catch with the ball.
3. They feel rain drops falling from the sky.
4. They run home quickly.
5. They both get wet.
6. Amanda had to change her clothes.
7. She hangs her wet clothes in the bathroom.
8. She goes to the kitchen.

Sequence 4:
1. Mother gives Amanda a snack.
2. Amanda cleans up her mess.
3. Father takes Amanda and Mother to a movie.
4. They buy popcorn and drinks.
5. Amanda sits in the movie theater.
6. She watches the movie.

7. Father drives his family home.
8. Amanda thanked them for a fun day.

More Practice Work for Chapter five using the same pictures.

Sequence 1: (*Note, this can be repeated for all 4 sequences.*)
Change each sentence to begin with I.
1. Amanda wakes up.
    I wake up.
2. She jumps out of bed.
    I jump out of bed.
3. She goes to the bathroom.
    I go to the bathroom.
4. She goes to the kitchen.
    I go to the kitchen.
5. Father cooks breakfast.
    I cook breakfast.
6. Amanda hugs her father.
    I hug my father.
7. She sits at the table.
    I sit at the table.
8. She eats pancakes.
    I eat pancakes.

Sequence 2: (*Note, this can be repeated for all 4 sequences.*)
End each sentence with *every Saturday*.
1. Amanda cleans the breakfast dishes *every Saturday*.
2. Mother takes Amanda to the mall *every Saturday*.
3. They shop for new shoes *every Saturday*.
4. They have lunch in the food court *every Saturday*.
5. They drive home *every Saturday*.
6. Amanda shows Father her new shoes *every Saturday*.
7. Father and Amanda go to the park *every Saturday*.
8. They get their ball gloves *every Saturday*.

Sequence 3 (*Note, this can be repeated for all 4 sequences.*)
Change each sentence to a question sentence.
1. Amanda plays on the swing.
     Does Amanda play on the swing?
2. Amanda and Father play catch with the ball.
     Do Amanda and Father play catch with the ball?
3. They feel rain drops falling from the sky.
     Do they feel raindrops falling from the sky?
4. They run home quickly.
     Do they run home quickly?
5. They both get wet.
     Do they both get wet?
6. Amanda had to change her clothes.
     Does Amanda have to change her clothes?
7. She hangs her wet clothes in the bathroom.
     Does Amanda hang her wet clothes in the bathroom?
8. She goes to the kitchen.
     Does Amanda go to the kitchen?

Sequence 4: (*Note, this can be repeated for all 4 sequences.*)
Change sentence 1 & 2, 3 & 4, etc. to a compound sentence using "and then".
1. Mother gives Amanda a snack.
2. Amanda cleans up her mess.
     Mother gives Amanda a snack and then Amanda cleans up her mess.
3. Father takes Amanda and Mother to a movie.
4. They buy popcorn and drinks.
     Father takes Amanda and mother to a movie and then they buy popcorn and drinks.
5 Amanda sits in the movie theater.
6. She watches the movie.
     Amanda sits in the movie theater and then watches the movie.
7. Father drives his family home.
8. Amanda thanked them for a fun day.
     Father drives his family home and then Amanda thanked them for a fun day.

MORE CONVERSATION:

1. What do you do on Saturday?
2. Do you go to the Mall?
3. What do you buy at the Mall?
4. Do you go to the movies?
5. What is your favorite movie?

APPENDIX

Grammar Helps

Simple first and third person – subject and verb agreement:

First person:
When you write in first person, you are talking about yourself. Singular (I) Plural(We).

Third person:
When you write in third person, you are talking about other people or characters without mentioning yourself. Singular(He/She) Plural(They)

I, You, They, We	wake, turn, get, put, go, wash, brush, make, pull, get, return, dress
Mother, Amanda, She/He/It	wakes, turns, gets, puts, goes, washes, brushes, makes, pulls, gets

I <u>wake</u> up in the morning.

     She _____ up in the morning.

     They _____ up in the morning.

     We _____ up in the morning.

I <u>turn</u> on the radio.

     She _____ on the radio.

     They _____ on the radio.

     Mother _____ on the radio.

I <u>wash</u> the clothes.

     She _____ the clothes.

     They _____ the clothes.

Mother _____ the clothes.

Adverbs of time:

Adverbs that change or qualify the meaning of a sentence by telling us when things happen are defined as **adverbs** of **time**. An **adverb** of **time** is just what you might expect it to be – a word that describes when, for how long, or how often a certain action happened.

In the morning tells when something is happening.

In the morning
In the afternoon
In the evening

Every day tells how often things happen. Is it one day? Two days? or Every day? which could equal 7 days a week.

Every day
Every night

Every morning
Every afternoon
Every evening

Adverbs of Time List

After reading this list of adverbs of time, you may be able to come up with several more on your own. Remember that adverbs of time always tell us when, how long, and how often something happens.

When: Yesterday – Today – Tomorrow – Later – Last year – Now

How Long: All morning – For hours – Since last week

How often: Frequently – Never – Sometimes – Often – Annually

Changing Positive to Negative

In the simple present tense, we make negative forms by putting **'not'** after **'do'** or **'does'**. Note that 'do' is used when the subject is a plural noun or pronoun. The first person pronoun 'I' also takes the verb 'do'. 'Does' is used when the subject is a singular noun or pronoun.

In the simple past tense, we make negatives by putting **'did not'** before the base form of the verb.

Read the following and say the correct word for the blank:

> 1. My sister .... not live with my parents. (do / does?)

> 2. I .... not know the answer. (do / does?)

> 3. I .... not want to leave now. (do / does?)

In speaking, contractions are acceptable. Even if you never use them, you should understand what they are because many people use them and you want to understand what they are saying.

A **contraction** consists of two words that are combined to form one word. To "contract" means to "**make** smaller," and that is what we do when we form **contractions**: we take two longer words and contract them into one shorter word.

Do not = Don't

Does not = Doesn't

Re-read the above three sample sentences and say the correct contraction.

Other examples of often used contractions:

Have not = Haven't

Has not = Hasn't

Is not = isn't

Are not = aren't

Can not = can't - The o sound in **not is** dropped and the letter o (no in the case of cannot) **is** replaced with an apostrophe.

Will Not = won't - **.will not** => won't drops ill from **will** and replaces it with the o from **not**. This **contraction is** probably derived from shifts in speech rather than writing.

Changing a Sentence to a Question

A sentence that tells us something is a statement. One way it can be changed into a question is to use **do, does or did** as the first word and ends with a question mark (?). Also the verb will change to agree with the subject.

An example is given below.

- My sister <u>enjoys</u> walking. (Statement)

- Does my sister <u>enjoy</u> walking? (Question)

Make question sentences from the following statements using **do, does or did.**

1. _____ mother <u>like</u> to bake cakes?

2. _____ you **call** your friend?

3. _____ I <u>meet</u> your mother yesterday?

Change all four of the above sentences to a statement followed by a period. (The underlined verbs will need to be changed to make the statement correct.)

1. _____

2. _____

3. _____

4. _____

Composing Compound Sentences:

There are mainly three kinds of sentences in English: **simple, complex** and **compound.**

Simple sentence

A simple sentence consists of just one clause. Examples are given below.

- The dog barks.

- The kettle boils.

- Birds live in nests.

- The boys are singing.

In its simplest form, a simple sentence consists of a subject and a verb.

Compound sentence

A compound sentence is made up of two or more independent sentences.

- The boys sang and the girls danced.

This compound sentence consists of two simple sentences connected by the coordinating conjunction **and.**

We make compound sentences by joining independent clauses with the help of coordinating conjunctions.

Two independent clauses need to be connected with a **coordinating conjunction** or separated with a full stop or a semicolon.

Here are some examples of coordinating conjunctions in English and what they do:

- **For** – presents rationale

- **And** – presents non-contrasting item(s) or idea(s)

- **Nor** – presents a non-contrasting negative idea

- **But** – presents a contrast or exception

- **Or** – presents an alternative item or idea

- **Yet** – presents a contrast or exception

- **So** – presents a consequence

Turn the following independent sentences into one sentence using the coordinating conjunction "and."

1. The time is 2:00 PM. The clock is ringing.

2. Today is Tuesday. It is raining.

3. The dog barked. He is loud.

4. The sky is blue. The grass is green.

5. The chair is big. The table is small.

Made in the USA
Monee, IL
17 March 2021